D1112181

Real People

Colin Powell

By Mary Hill

Children's Press®
A Division of Scholastic Inc.
New York / Toronto / London / Auckland / Sydney
Mexico City / New Delhi / Hong Kong
Danbury, Connecticut

Photo Credits: Cover, pp. 15, 21 © AFP/Corbis; p. 5 © Joseph Sohm/Chromosohm Inc./Corbis; p. 7 © David Turnley/Corbis; p. 9 © Peter Turnley/Corbis; p. 11 © Tim Shaffer/Reuters/TimePix; p. 13 © Reuters NewMedia Inc./Corbis; p. 17 © Wally McNamee/Corbis; p. 19 © AP/Wide World Photos
Contributing Editor: Jennifer Silate
Book Design: Daniel Hosek

Library of Congress Cataloging-in-Publication Data

Hill, Mary, 1977–
    Colin Powell / by Mary Hill.
    p. cm. — (Real people)
    Summary: An easy-to-read biography of General Colin Powell
    who, in 2001, became the first African American to be appointed
    secretary of state.
    Includes bibliographical references (p.) and index.
    ISBN 0-516-24288-1 (lib. bdg.) — ISBN 0-516-27885-1 (pbk.)
    1. Powell, Colin L.—Juvenile literature. 2. Statesmen—United
    States—Biography—Juvenile literature. 3. Generals—United
    States—Biography—Juvenile literature. 4. African American
    generals—Biography—Juvenile literature. 5. United States.
    Army—Biography—Juvenile literature. [1. Powell, Colin L. 2. Cabinet
    officers. 3. Generals. 4. African Americans—Biography.] I. Title. II.
    Series: Real people (Children's Press)

E840.8.P64 H55 2003
327.73'0092--dc21
                                                        2002152677

Contents

Meet Colin Powell.

Colin Powell works for the United States of America.

4

5

Colin Powell is **married** to Alma Johnson.

Colin Powell was a **general** in the United States **Army**.

Colin was given many **awards** for his **bravery**.

In 2001, President George W. Bush chose Colin to be the **secretary of state**.

Colin Powell is the first **African American** to ever have that job.

13

Colin Powell visits many countries.

He meets with the leaders of other countries.

15

Colin Powell also gives many **speeches** around the world.

He talks about making people's lives better.

Colin also works with groups that help children.

19

Colin Powell works hard to make the world a better place.

21

New Words

African American (**af**-ruh-kuhn uh-**mer**-uh-kuhn) someone who was born in the United States or became a U.S. citizen and can trace his or her ancestors back to Africa

army (**ar**-mee) a group of people who fight together during a war

awards (uh-**wordz**) prizes given to a person for doing something well

bravery (**brayv**-uhr-ee) strong and without fear

general (**jen**-ur-uhl) a very high-ranking officer in the army

married (**mar**-eed) having a husband or wife

secretary of state (**sek**-ruh-ter-ee **uhv stayt**) a person who advises the president of the United States on how to handle things with other countries

speeches (**speech**-uhz) talks given to groups of people

To Find Out More

Books
Colin Powell
by John Passaro
Childs World

Colin Powell: It Can Be Done!
by Mike Strong
Capstone Press

Web Site
General Powell's Corner
http://www.americaspromise.org/GenPowellCorner/
    GenPowellCorner.cfm
Read about Colin Powell and a letter he wrote to
the kids of America.

Index

About the Author
Mary Hill writes and edits children's books.

Reading Consultants
Kris Flynn, Coordinator, Small School District Literacy, The San Diego County
Office of Education

Shelly Forys, Certified Reading Recovery Specialist, W.J. Zahnow Elementary
School, Waterloo, IL

Sue McAdams, Former President of the North Texas Reading Council of the
IRA, and Early Literacy Consultant, Dallas, TX